By Request:

Songs

—for the—

Community of Christ

For additional information, contact Worship Ministries, The Auditorium, 1001 W. Walnut, Independence, MO 64050.

Independence, Missouri
Printed in the United States of America

ISBN 0-8309-1108-1

Preface

By Request: Songs for the Community of Christ offers the texts and music most often requested by you from the Worship Ministries department. It includes original work by several church members, as well as some favorites of past World Conferences. It is a blessing to be able to publish these gems for your creative use within the worship life of the church.

In addition to the Index found at the back of the book, there are also short statements about each song. These include stories of the creation of the songs and, in some cases, testimonies of the ministry the song has provided.

As we "prepare for and experience vibrant worship," may these songs be resources for worshiping God.

Worship Ministries
Jane M. Gardner
Jan Kraybill
Eileen Terril

R-1 This Is God's Wondrous World

TERRA BEATA S.M.D.

Text: Maltbie D. Babcock, 1858-1901, alt.
Tune: Traditional English Melody, adapted by Franklin L. Sheppard, 1852-1930.

R-2 Standing on the Promises

PROMISES 11.11.11.9.Ref.

Text amd Tune: R. Kelso Carter, 1891.

Refrain
Stand - - - ing, stand - - - ing,
Stand - ing on the prom - is - es, stand - ing on the prom - is - es,
stand - ing on the prom - is - es of God my Sav - ior;
stand - - - ing, stand - - - ing,
stand - ing on the prom - is - es, stand - ing on the prom - is - es,
I'm stand - ing on the prom - is - es of God.

R-3 Light Dawns on a Weary World

TEMPLE OF PEACE 7.6.6.7.8.12.11.12.11.

Text: Mary Louise Bringle, © 2002 GIA Publications, Inc., Chicago, Illinois.
Tune: William P. Rowan, © 2000 William P. Rowan, admin. GIA Publications, Inc.

clap their hands; the dry lands, gush with springs; the hills and
moun-tains shall break forth with sing-ing! We shall go out in joy, and be led
forth in peace, as all the world in won-der echo-es sha - lom.

R-4 Communion Prayers

BREAD (Spanish)

Text: Community of Christ Communion prayers, *Doctrine and Covenants* 17:22, 23.
Tune: Jan Kraybill and John Glaser, arr. Jan Kraybill.

Dm11 C B♭ Am G Dm7
to - dos los que par - ti - ci - pan de él, que lo co - man en me -
C2/E F G G/F G/E Dm
mo - ria del cuer - po de tu Hi - jo, y te den tes - ti - mo-nio, oh
C/E Gsus4 G (NC) C Dm C/E
Dios, Pa - dre E-ter - no, de que de - sean to - mar so - bre

F G Am Bb Am
sí el nom-bre de tu Hi-jo y a-cor-dar-se siem-pre de
Ab C/G FM7 C/E
Él, y guar-dar Sus man-da-mien-tos que Él les ha da-do, a
Am G Fsus2 F Dm7 C2
fin de que siem-pre ten-gan Su Es-pi-rí-tu con-si-go. A-men.
rit. to end

WINE (English)

G
Dm7
C2/E
that they may do it in re - mem - brance of the
F
G
G/F G/E
Dm
C/E
Gsus4
blood of thy Son which was shed for
G
(NC)
3
C
Dm
C/E
them, that they may wit - ness un - to thee, O

F G Am B♭
God, the e-ter-nal Fath - er, that they do al - ways re -
Am A♭ C/G FMaj7
mem-ber him, that they may have his Spir - it to be with
C/E Am G Fsus2 F Dm7 C2
them. A - men, A - men, and A - men, A - men.

R-5 God of All

SEPTEMBER 11TH 8.8.9.7.8.5.8.5

Text: Randall and Mary Pratt. *Tune:* Randall and Mary Pratt, arr. Jan Kraybill.

hands, [Isaiah 2:2-4] From death to life You raise Your
chil - dren, [John 11:25] God of All, bless ev - 'ry land. [Matthew 5:45]
rit.
a tempo
1. God of Love, how can we
2. God of Light, shine in our
3. God of Truth, we trust Your
rit.
a tempo

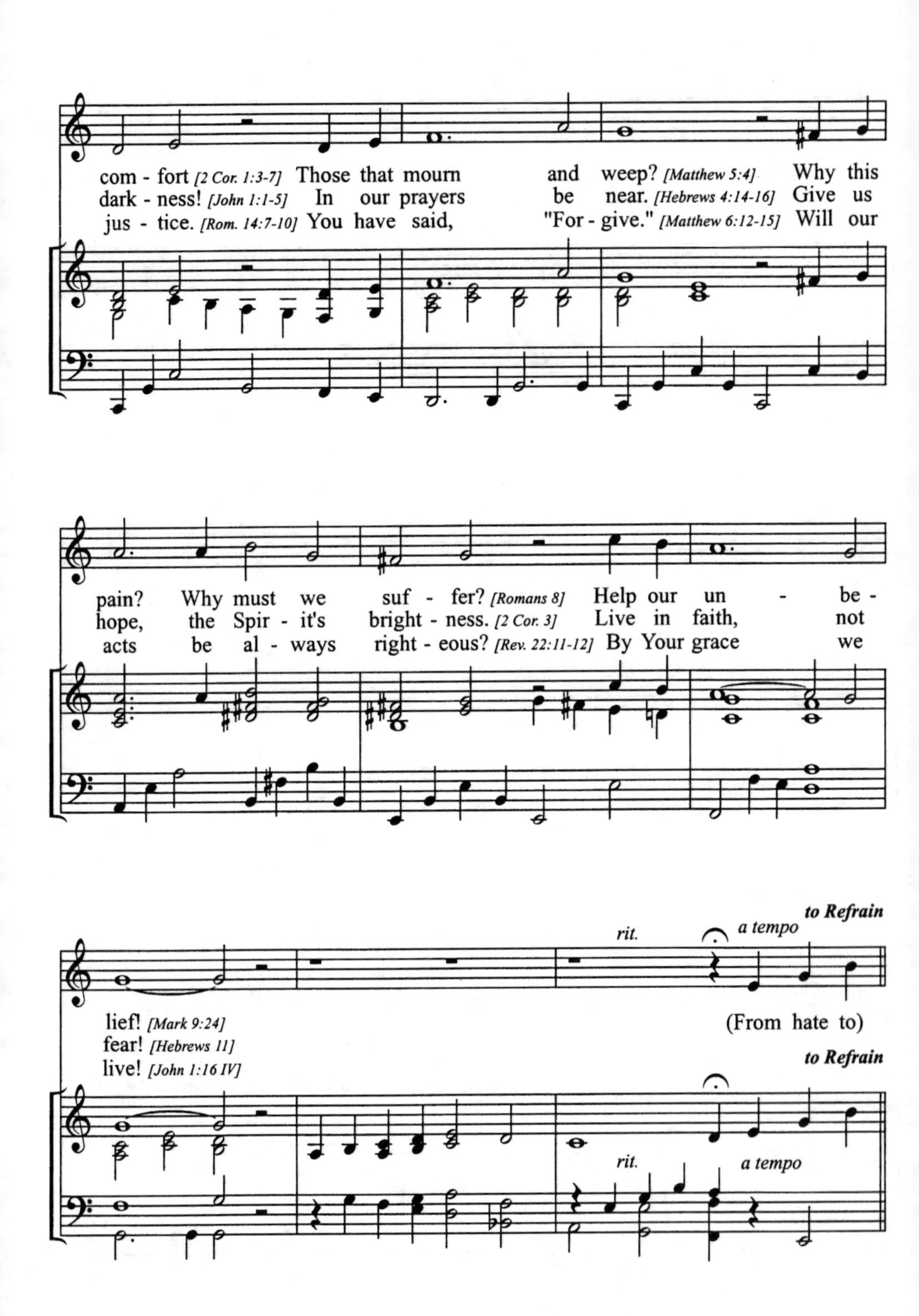

com - fort [2 Cor. 1:3-7] Those that mourn and weep? [Matthew 5:4] Why this
dark - ness! [John 1:1-5] In our prayers be near. [Hebrews 4:14-16] Give us
jus - tice. [Rom. 14:7-10] You have said, "For - give." [Matthew 6:12-15] Will our
pain? Why must we suf - fer? [Romans 8] Help our un - be -
hope, the Spir - it's bright - ness. [2 Cor. 3] Live in faith, not
acts be al - ways right - eous? [Rev. 22:11-12] By Your grace we
rit.
a tempo
to Refrain
lief! [Mark 9:24]
fear! [Hebrews 11]
live! [John 1:16 IV]
(From hate to)
to Refrain
rit.
a tempo

R-6 When Law and Love in Tension Lie

C Dm/G Csus C
lib - er - ate each soul con - fined, Sweep
reach - ing those who cry in need, En -
those whom God has giv - en birth To
high - er hopes and no - bler talk. For
Dm7 Em7
from our hearts in - ordi - nate care of
large our hearts, ex - pand our dreams, re -
life that's not con - ven - tion– tied nor
love, the "al - pha - bet of grace," spells
FMaj7 Dm Em F Em/G
self, and place, and stat - utes fair To
lease our grip on safe - ty's chains So
squelched by fel - low - ship de - nied. Flood
out the dream that ev - ery race Shall

Am Em F C Am
sac - ri - fice these less - er claims in
we may dwell in sa - cred space where
then our souls with new re - solve to
live in God's com - mu - ni - ty en -
Gm F
1-3
B♭ Gsus G
lieu of one that bears God's name.
2. When
love is viewed in ev - ery face.
3. Let
o - pen doors where hurts dis - solve.
4. Help
riched by faith's di–
4
B♭ Gm7 C
ver - si - ty!

R-7 Kum ba yah

Traditional spiritual

Text and Tune: arranged by Romina Mootua; transcribed by Jan Kraybill.

I
II
Kum ba, Kum ba, Kum ba, Kum ba Kum ba yah Kum ba, Kum ba, Kum ba,
III
Kum ba, Kum ba, Kum ba, Kum ba yah Kum ba, Kum ba, Kum ba,
Sp.
Kum ba, uh-uh, m Kum ba, uh - uh, m Kum ba, uh - uh, m

I
Kum ba
II
Kum ba Kum ba yah Kum ba, Kum ba, Kum ba, Kum ba Kum ba yah
III
Kum ba yah Kum ba, Kum ba, Kum ba, Kum ba yah
Sp.
Kum ba, uh - uh, m Kum ba, uh-uh, m Kum ba, uh - uh, m

I
yah, my Lord, Kum ba yah.
II
Kum ba, Kum ba, Kum ba, Kum ba Kum ba yah Kum ba, Kum ba, Kum ba,
III
Kum ba, Kum ba, Kum ba, Kum ba yah Kum ba, Kum ba, Kum ba,
Sp.
Kum ba, uh - uh, m Kum ba, uh - uh, m Kum ba, uh-uh, m

I
Kum ba yah, my Lord, Kum ba
II
Kum ba Kum ba yah Kum ba, Kum ba, Kum ba, Kum ba Kum ba yah
III
Kum ba yah Kum ba, Kum ba, Kum ba, Kum ba yah
Sp.
Kum ba, uh - uh, m Kum ba, uh - uh, m Kum ba, uh - uh, m

I
yah.
Kum ba yah, my Lord,
II
Kum ba, Kum ba, Kum ba, Kum ba Kum ba yah Kum ba, Kum ba, Kum ba,
III
Kum ba, Kum ba, Kum ba, Kum ba yah Kum ba, Kum ba, Kum ba,
Sp.
Kum ba, uh-uh, m Kum ba, uh - uh, m Kum ba, uh - uh, m

I
Kum ba yah.
II
Kumba Kumbayah Kum ba, Kum ba, Kum ba, Kum ba Kum ba yah
III
Kumba yah Kum ba, Kum ba, Kum ba, Kum ba yah
Sp.
Kumba, uh - uh, m Kum ba, uh - uh, m Kum ba, uh - uh, m

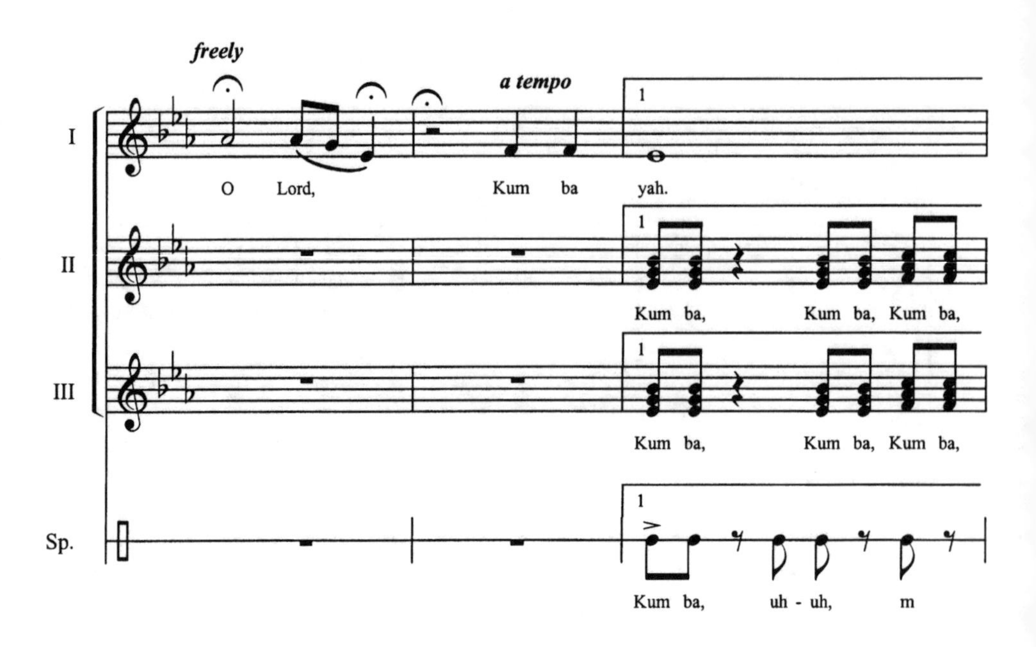
freely
a tempo
I
II
III
Sp.
1
O Lord,
Kum ba
yah.
Kum ba, Kum ba, Kum ba,
Kum ba, Kum ba, Kum ba,
Kum ba, uh - uh, m

I
II
III
Sp.
2
yah.
Kum ba Kum ba yah
Kum ba, Kum ba, Kum ba, Kum ba Kum ba yah
Kum ba yah
Kum ba, Kum ba, Kum ba, Kum ba yah
Kum ba, uh - uh, m
Kum ba, uh-uh, m
Kum ba, uh - uh, m

I
II
Kum ba, Kum ba, Kum ba, Kum ba Kum ba yah Kum ba, Kum ba, Kum ba,
III
Kum ba, Kum ba, Kum ba, Kum ba yah Kum ba, Kum ba, Kum ba,
Sp.
Kum ba, uh-uh, m Kum ba, uh - uh, m Kum ba, uh-uh, m

I
II
Kumba Kumba yah Kumba, Kumba,Kumba, Kum ba Kumba yah
III
Kumba yah Kumba, Kumba,Kumba, Kum ba yah
Sp.
Kumba, uh - uh, m Kumba, uh-uh, m Kumba, uh-uh, m Kumba!

R-8 Rain Down

Refrain
F A7 G/B A7 Dm F7 E♭/G F7/A
Rain down, rain down,
B♭ F/A Gm7 C7 Gm7/D C7/E
rain down your love on your peo - - ple.
F A7 Dm F7 E♭/G F7/A
Rain down, rain down,
3
3
B♭ Am7 Gm7 Gm/C Am/C Gm/C B♭/F F
rain down your love, God of life.

F A7 Dm F7 E♭/G F7/A
1. Faith - ful and true is the word of our God.
2. We who re - vere and find hope in our God
3. God of cre - a - tion, we long for your truth;
B♭ F/A G7 C7 B♭/D C7/E
All of God's works are so wor - thy of trust.
live in the kind - ness and joy of God's wing.
you are the wa - ter of life that we thirst.
F A7 Dm F7
God's mer - cy falls on the just and the right;
God will pro - tect us from dark - ness and death;
Grant that your love and your peace touch our hearts;
to Refrain
B♭ Gm7 Gm/C Am/C Gm/C F C B♭/D C7/E
full of God's love is the earth.
God will not leave us to starve.
all of our hope lies in you.

R-9 All Are Called

R-10 I Have Called You by Your Name

Text and Tune: Daniel Charles Damon,

R-11 Community of Christ

Text and Tune: Jay Goos. A gift from Jay Goos to the Community of Christ, 2002.

B♭
F
least of us should stum - ble, We all feel the pain: Com-
peace be-tween the na - tions And love be-tween us all; Com-
Saints of ev - ery na - tion Rise a - gain, to die no more: A com-
least of us should stum - ble, We all feel the pain: Com-
C
C7
1, 2, 3
F
mu-ni - ty of Christ is our name. 2. We are a
mu-ni - ty of Christ is our call. 3. We are a
mu-ni - ty of Christ forev-er - more! 4. We are a
mu-ni - ty of Christ is our
4
F
name.

R-12 Christ Leads!

SPES 2.6.6.2.6.6.6.3.

Text: Brian Wren, © 2001 by Hope Publishing Company, Carol Stream, IL 60188, USA.
 Tune: Thomas Brown, © 2001 Community of Christ Copyright Corporation.

and the clam - or of change
and the an - ger of need
and com - mu - ni - ty praise
at the ul - ti - mate end,
Christ Je - sus
Christ Je - sus
Christ Je - sus
Christ Je - sus
is our guide.
speaks to - day.
makes us one.
lives and leads.
God be praised!
God be praised! (to vs. 3)
God be praised!
God be praised!

3. Christ waits! Cru - ci - fied by the pow'rs,

un - de - feat - ed, a - live, Christ waits.
To the wor - ship of force and the praise of re -
venge Christ Je - sus teach - es peace. God be praised!

This page intentionally left blank to avoid awkward page turns.

R-13 Christ Leads!

Text: Brian Wren, © 2001 by Hope Publishing Company, Carol Stream, IL 60188, USA.

Tune: John R. Kleinheksel, Sr., © 2001 Community of Christ Copyright Corporation.

F
Em7
Dm7
G7
clam - or of change Christ Je - sus is our guide.
an - ger of need Christ Je - sus speaks to - day.
praise of re - venge Christ Je - sus teach - es peace.
mu - ni - ty praise Christ Je - sus makes us one.
ul - ti - mate end, Christ Je - sus lives and leads.
Dm7
G7
C
1-4
God be praised!
God be praised!
God be praised!
God be praised!
God be
1-4
5
praised!
5

R-14 Community of Christ

LEONI 6.6.8.4.D.

Text: Shirley Erena Murray, © 1992 Hope Publishing Company, Carol Stream, IL 60188.

Tune: Hebrew melody, arr. Meyer Lyon, 1751-1797.

R-15 Put Peace into Each Other's Hands

ST. COLUMBA 8.7.8.7.

Text: Fred Kaan, *Tune:* Traditional Irish melody.

R-16 Community of Joy, Proclaim the Living Christ!

DARWALL'S 148th 6.6.6.6.8.8.

Text: Kenneth L. McLaughlin,
Tune: John Darwall, 1731-1789.

R-17 We Have the Power to Share the Light

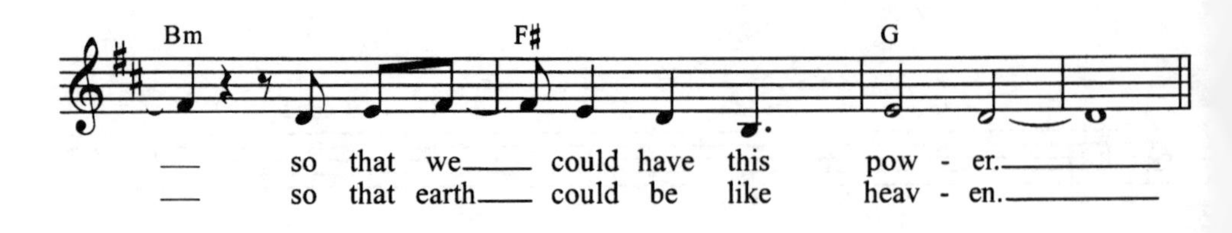

Chorus:

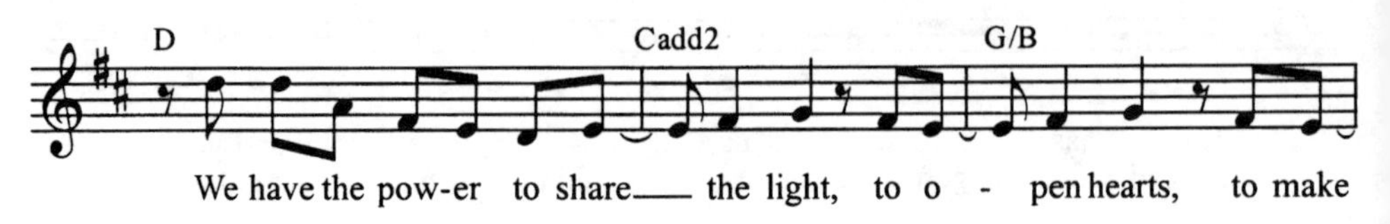

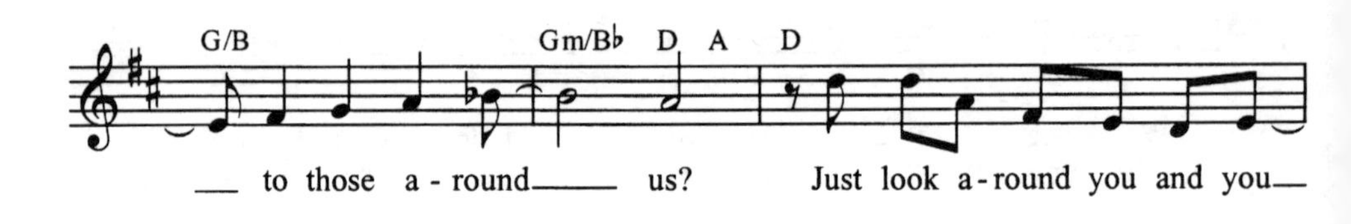

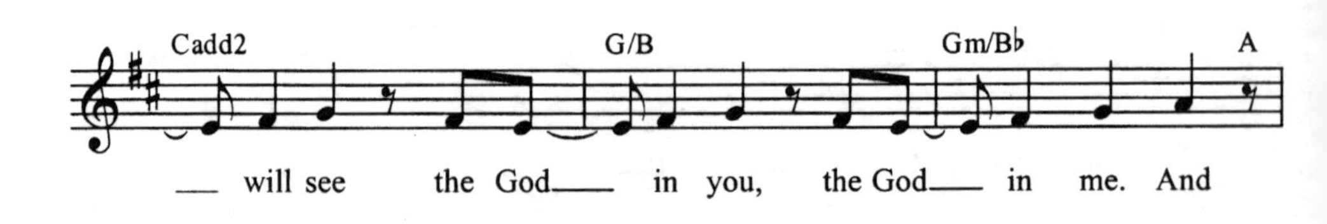

Third time to Coda

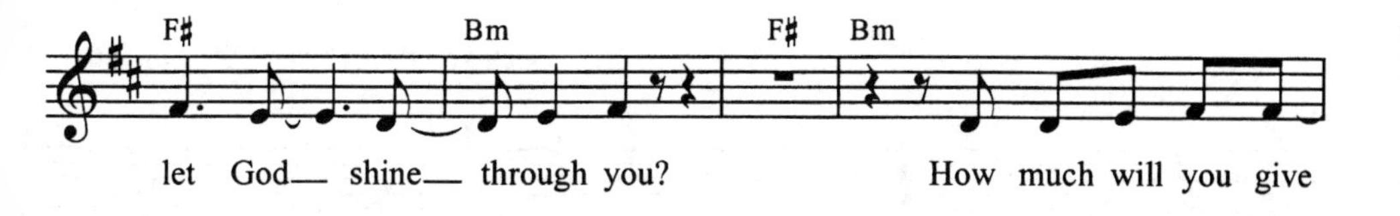
F♯ Bm F♯ Bm
let God shine through you? How much will you give

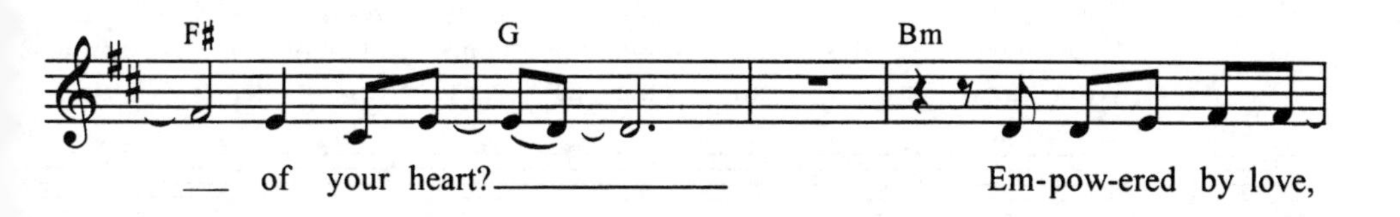
F♯ G Bm
of your heart? Em-pow-ered by love,

F♯ 3 Bm F♯ Bm
Je-sus gave ev-'ry - thing. And out of that love,

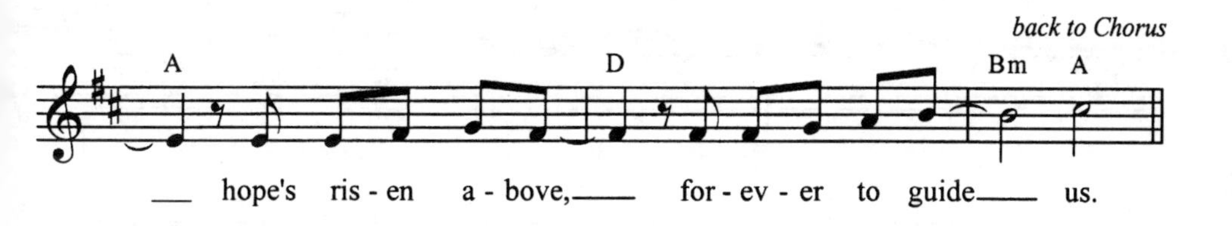
back to Chorus
A D Bm A
hope's ris-en a-bove, for-ev-er to guide us.

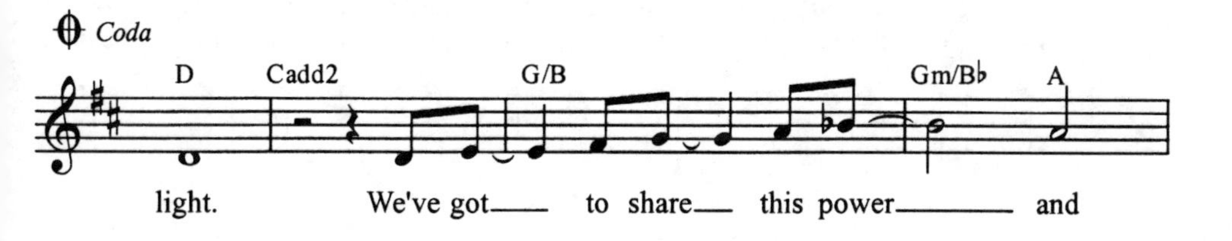
Coda
D Cadd2 G/B Gm/B♭ A
light. We've got to share this power and

D Cadd2 G/B Gm/B♭ A D
light. We need to share this power and light.

R-18 The Spirit of God Like a Fire Is Burning

PARACLETE 12.11.12.11. with refrain

Text: W.W. Phelps, 1792-1872; original stanza 3 and chorus alt. by Andrew Bolton and Randall Pratt,
 Tune: English Tune.

Refrain
We'll sing and we'll shout with the {an - gels / ar - mies} of heav - en,
"Ho - san - nah, ho - san - nah to God and the Lamb!"
Let glo - ry to them in the high - est be giv - en
Hence - forth and for - ev - er! A - men, and a - men!

R-19 Take the Path of the Disciple

TAKE THE PATH 8.7.8.7.D.

Text: Randall Pratt. *Tune:* Randall Pratt, arr. Janet Kraybill.

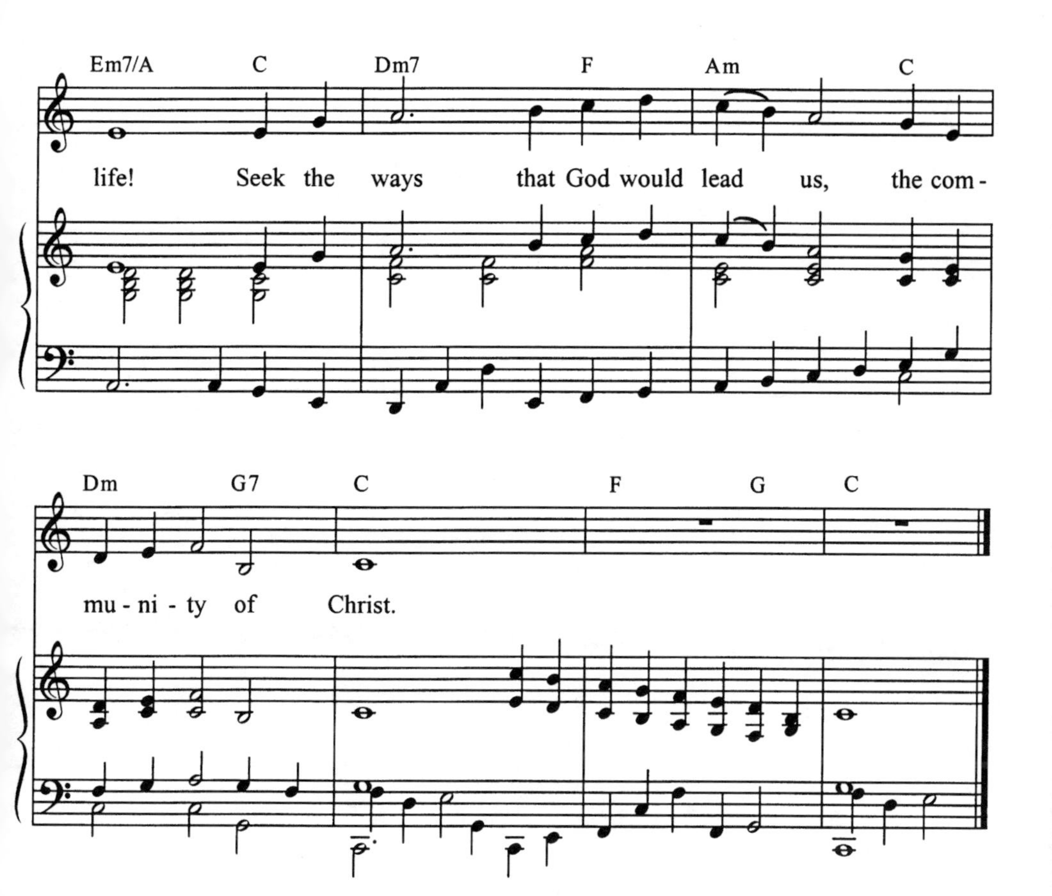
Em7/A
C
Dm7
F
Am
C
life! Seek the ways that God would lead us, the com-
Dm
G7
C
F
G
C
mu - ni - ty of Christ.

By Request: Songs for the Community of Christ

R-1 This Is God's Wondrous World

This is an inclusive-language modification of the beloved hymn, "This Is My Father's World." In the latter part of the nineteenth century, the author of the original words took early morning walks up a hill that overlooked beautiful Lake Ontario. As he left his home he would say, "I'm going out to see my Father's world." This new version was discovered in a delightful book *Joyful Noise: Songs of Faith and Fun for Children* and included in the 2002 World Conference hymnal.

R-2 Standing on the Promises

Principal Conductor Jack Ergo selected this song as part of the 1996 World Conference hymn festival, arranging it for orchestra and large choir. It is a favorite hymn of his wife, Jolia. It was also sung as part of the 1997 Elders and Leaders Conference and subsequent Congregational Leaders Workshops. Although not found in our denominational hymnody, it is widely enjoyed in other parts of the ecumenical community. Originally written in the late 1800s, the gospel-style harmonies and theology of "God as Protector" make it both fun to sing and worthy of remembrance.

R-3 Light Dawns on a Weary World

Community of Christ has a long-term relationship with the Hymn Society in the United States and Canada. Worship Ministries staff were thrilled to host the 2001 Hymn Society annual conference at the Temple and Auditorium. This group of Christian authors, composers, academicians, and church musicians from throughout North America spent a week in Independence singing, worshiping, and learning. One particularly challenging message, titled "Peacemaking through Worship," was offered by Fred Kaan, a prominent hymn-text author passionate about peace-and-justice issues.

At the next year's annual conference in Winston-Salem, North Carolina, the Worship Ministries executives were astounded and moved to hear Mary Louise Bringle, a professor and hymn-text author from Brevard College in North Carolina, describe her experience during the previous year's conference in Independence. She then introduced her breathtaking hymn, "Light Dawns on a Weary World," which she had written in her hotel room in reaction to Fred Kaan's presentation a year earlier in the "Peace Temple." The refrain is a paraphrase of Isaiah 55. The tune's composer, William Rowan, also participated in the 2001 conference in the Temple and named his composition, "Temple of Peace."

R-4 Communion Prayers

Although Community of Christ worship is largely "free form"—little is actually liturgically required—prayers are prescribed to be offered over the Communion bread and wine. Those words are found in Community of Christ's Doctrine and Covenants. In the continuing effort to make World Conference worships as ethnically inclusive and symbolically touching as possible, the 2002 planning committee requested that these prayers be sung in Spanish and English. Musician John Glaser and Principal Organist Jan Kraybill were charged with composing tunes to fit the words of the prayers.

The prayer over the wine is sung in Spanish and the one over the bread in English. Both tunes have the same melodic contours but, working with the challenges of setting translated texts to music, were designed to fit the speech patterns of the languages. If a musician is very creative and uses the melody as a loose guide, other languages could also be used with the tunes.

R-5 God of All

Randall Pratt and Mary Pratt wrote this text in response to the tragedy of September 11, 2001, and offered it both as a worship resource and healing gift. In the September 2002 *Herald* they wrote, "There is such a temptation, politically and culturally, to pattern our thoughts and actions from our myth of redemptive violence—the myth that our response should be to seek destruction of 'the evildoers.' This is certainly not the way of Christ. This hymn is about God's love for *all* and action to redeem *all*. It also speaks to how we should process experiences of violence and terror in a faithful way—not just

September 11, but all acts that result in pain and hurt." The scripture references noted between the phrases guide toward words of love and peace found in the Bible.

When Randall Pratt and Jan Kraybill began working on the musical accompaniment to his tune, he suggested the arrangement begin with a horrific musical "crash" symbolizing the shock of the physical airline crashes into the twin towers. The next notes calmly "fall"—the floating of millions of pieces of paper—the music coming to rest in quiet, cold reflection. The music of the stanzas and refrain is reflective, appropriately reminding us of God's loving care in times of hurt and pain. "God of All" was premiered at a Kansas City–area interfaith service satellite broadcast from the Auditorium commemorating the first anniversary of the 9/11 tragedies.

R-6 When Law and Love in Tension Lie

Presiding Evangelist Danny Belrose comments on his text which calls all to accountability:

> Sometimes social, philosophical, and theological constructs become binding. Rules, regulations, and religious interpretations take on a life of their own. Quick to accuse the Pharisees of unhealthy adherence to laws they deemed sacrosanct—we are slow to see how subtly we mirror their rigidity. There are times when we face ethical dilemmas where competing values cry for a decision. We live in a world (and a culture) of diverse understandings of what is right and wrong. What do we do when pressed to decide between opposing interests—when we are torn between "lawgiver and pastor"? How do we respond in circumstances where, in Paul's words, we must "rightly divide the word of truth"? Well, we do the best we can. We prioritize. We sacrifice. One value is sacrificed for another as we reach for the greatest good. This hymn expresses this tension and the desire to see "law" and "love" as equal partners.

Randall Pratt wrote the tune for this hymn to amplify the power of the text, and titled it PRAYTRIARCH in honor of its author.

R-7 Kum ba yah

This Tahitian arrangement breathes new life into a well-known campfire song. Arranged by Romina Mootua, it was taught to youth ministers Tim Dodds and Chad Godfrey while they were providing ministry in the islands. It is very popular among the children and youth in Tahiti, and Chad says, "Once we learned it, we knew immediately that it needed to be recorded and included on the CD, and to be taught to North American youth."

The song is found on the CD *Te E'a O Te Hau—The Path of Peace,* which accompanied the church's camp helps in 2002, and the Power and Light 2003 CD *You Have the Power to Share the Light.* This arrangement utilizes multiple voice parts, solo voice, and a spoken percussive part, and may be accompanied with various hand percussion instruments.

R-8 Rain Down

"Rain Down" was sung at a 2002 World Conference worship service that highlighted water, light, and wind as symbols of the Spirit. It quotes scripture using the analogy of justice falling like rain, and is quickly becoming an ecumenical favorite.

Born in New York and raised in El Salvador, composer Jaime Cortez was exposed to a diversity of music that influences his work. His approach to music and to the diversity of cultures present in congregations is to "share, celebrate, and honor other cultures." Whether it is in food or music, he exclaims, "Let's bring all our gifts together!"

R-9 All Are Called

About this hymn, enjoyed at the 1997 Elders and Leaders Conference, author Presiding Evangelist Danny Belrose writes,

> The keynote of "All Are Called" is diversity! We live in many worlds. We have unique histories, rich cultural traditions, and differing political systems and laws. Diversity is a blessing, not a curse. Unity does not mean conformity, but cries instead for mutual respect of our God-given connection—a reverence for our shared humanity and the created order. Diversity kisses unity

when we strip away lines that separate our togetherness. We *are* inextricably connected—irrevocably part of the family of God. Unity is not an exercise in having others see our way—but an adventure in finding God's way. It has to do with being *for others* as well as *with others*—the acknowledgment that if I am *for me*, I must be *for you*!

R-10 I Have Called You by Your Name

Isaiah 43:1 NRSV exclaims, "But now thus says the LORD, he who created you, O Jacob, he who formed you, O Israel: Do not fear, for I have redeemed you; I have called you by name, you are mine."

Basing his song on this scripture, Dan Damon wrote this text for his own ordination. An internationally published and prolific writer of spiritually-crafted hymn texts and tunes, Dan also shepherds a small Methodist congregation in California.

This hymn was published in the book distributed to Community of Christ congregations for the denomination's name change in 2001 and sung by Graceland University Concert Choir in the service commemorating that change in the Temple on April 6, 2001. It was also sung at an ordination service during World Conference 2002. Its poignant text carries a powerful message appropriate for ordination services and any worship in which God's call is celebrated.

R-11 Community of Christ (Goos)

In 2002 R. Jay Goos sent a letter to both church President Grant McMurray and Worship Ministries with a CD that contained a song. It said in part,

> You don't know me, and I am not a member of your denomination. However, in the past six months, the Community of Christ CyberCongregation has come to mean a lot to me, particularly during a time of crisis of my daughter's health last spring. I took in a part of your World Conference via Web cast, particularly Mr. McMurray's keynote speech. Also, about a month ago, I was visiting my sister in Kansas City, and I spent some time praying in your Temple.

> Even though I am not a member of your tradition, I think that I have caught a glimpse of what your church stands for, and where your leadership wants the church to go. I thought that it was worth honoring in a song... I felt a calling on my heart to give something back to the Community of Christ, and, in writing and donating a song to your church, I feel I have fulfilled my charge.
>
> Sincerely, R. Jay Goos, Fargo, North Dakota

The song has taken off among Community of Christ CyberCongregation members and others. According to theologian-in-residence Anthony Chvala-Smith, it "aptly and insightfully sums up who we are and are becoming. Sometimes it seems that an 'outside' voice can help us more than anything else to hear and sense what's really going on among us. This hymn offers such a voice." A song reaching out to our Christian community, through the efforts of the CyberCongregation, it has already been translated into multiple languages.

R-12 Christ Leads! (Brown)

Brian Wren is one of the world's premier living hymn authors. Community of Christ worship personnel have a long relationship with Dr. Wren, so when the idea arose to commission a hymn for Worship '01—a worship seminar held at the Temple in the summer of 2001—his name was top on the list. Brian shaped his text around this denomination's heritage, theology, and mission. After the text was received, a search was launched for a tune to complement the touching words. Of eighty-three submissions, the tune called SPES (meaning "hope") by Thomas Brown was felt by the committee to most embody the text's call. Tom Brown is a distinguished organist and has served as a staff organist at Community of Christ headquarters for many years. The new hymn was debuted at Worship '01 and also introduced that year at the annual conference of the Hymn Society in the United States and Canada. The text and tune have been chosen to appear in a new collection of Wren's work produced by Hope Publishing Company in summer 2004.

R-13 Christ Leads! (Kleinheksel)

The text is the same as found in R-12. See above for text information.

This tune, by John Kleinheksel, placed second in the tune competition to match Brian Wren's commissioned text. The committee felt this tune also fit Wren's text well and showcased a different musical style, so it wanted to give congregations the option of using the Wren text with either tune.

R-14 Community of Christ (Murray)

Shirley Erena Murray is a renowned New Zealand hymn-text author with works published and enjoyed all over the globe. Her hymns address such themes as the unity for the church, women, human rights, justice, peace, and the integrity of creation. "Community of Christ" was first officially sung at the General Assembly of the Presbyterian Church of New Zealand in 1985. A hymn on social justice, it embodies many of the causes to which the denomination now bearing this name remains dedicated.

R-15 Put Peace into Each Other's Hands

Fred Kaan is a world-renowned hymn-text author who is passionate about pragmatic peace-and-justice issues. The original version of this text is found in *Sing for Peace*. Although it was written to be used at Communion services, in Kaan's native England it became traditionally used at an annual hospice service, so he wrote alternate verses making the text more ecumenical and less specific for Communion. He now prefers these words be used when this hymn is sung.

R-16 Community of Joy, Proclaim the Living Christ!

Apostle Ken McLaughlin wrote this text in Estes Park, Colorado at the YMCA of the Rockies during a retreat of the Joint Council in 1994. He explains:

> Much of the time spent at the retreat was centered on the creation of the mission statement of the church, which was birthed in the midst of the strong, creative

presence of the Holy Spirit. After the mission statement was completed, the Joint Council unexpectedly moved into another creative period in which the name Community of Christ emerged—reflecting, of course, the focal identity of our denomination: the proclamation of Jesus Christ in all that we say, do, and are; and the promotion of the cause of Zion, contemporarily called community.

The first four verses of the text were written in a matter of hours over a period of two days and with the tune firmly in mind. The last verse was added later, for use at World Conference. The penning of this text was perhaps the most pleasurable of all my writing experiences. It was birthed in joy.

R-17 We Have the Power to Share the Light

Forefront Ministries asked church Field Specialist and musician Kevin Henrickson to write the title track of the 2003 CD *You Have the Power to Share the Light*, designed to accompany the Power and Light curriculum for children, youth, and adults. It conveys the joy of being empowered by God to share the message of Christ's ministry and love.

The accompaniment on the lead sheet was designed to be used by guitarists and praise bands rather than keyboardists, as is appropriate for this musical style. The rhythms are a driving force in this song and at the same time relaxed from the beat. Notated on paper these syncopations look harder than they actually are when sung. Listen to the CD for a model to follow.

R-18 The Spirit of God Like a Fire Is Burning

This hymn, which has been called the "anthem" of the Community of Christ denomination, was sung at the dedication of Kirtland Temple in 1836. While use of the hymn in recent years has only included three stanzas, the first hymnal of the church, Emma Smith's 1835 hymnbook, included six stanzas, with this the last:

How blessed the day when the lamb and the lion
Shall lie down together without any ire;

And Ephraim be crown'd with his blessing in Zion
As Jesus descends with his chariots of fire!

Peace and Justice Minister Andrew Bolton hopes to reclaim this stanza for the present day to remind all of God's call for peace and justice as found in Isaiah 11:6. With Randall Pratt, the stanza was altered to speak more clearly to this call and the hope of Zion. The word "angels" was added as an alternative to "armies" in the chorus, symbolic of the diversity of stewardship within the church for seeking peace. The altered hymn was first sung at the 2002 World Conference hymn festival.

R-19 Take the Path of the Disciple

One morning in October 2000, author Randall Pratt was reflecting on a project exploring what "justice" might mean as he and other ministers embraced deeper discipleship in the Community of Christ. The tune and words "Take the path of the disciple" urgently spoke to him. The Spirit pressed him until the completed text and melody were down on paper and mailed to Jan Kraybill in Worship Ministries. The song arrived the very morning of a meeting planning the worship services leading up to the church's name change in April 2001. Jan composed the accompaniment, and it was included in the name change congregational resource book, sung at the inaugural name change worship service by the Graceland University Concert Choir, and also enjoyed at the 2002 World Conference. Its words inspire the denomination to continue to follow the Path of the Disciple described by President W. Grant McMurray in his address to the World Conference in 2000.

Index

**Community of Christ author, composer, and/or arranger*